The Curious Guide to
THINGS
THAT AREN'T

Walter Foster
Jr.

BY JOHN D. FIXX AND JAMES F. FIXX

ILLUSTRATED BY ABBY CARTER

There are many things that
aren't really things at all.

Sometimes, you can't touch them,
smell them, or put them in a box.
Often, you can't even see them.

This is a book about
the things that aren't.

Can you guess
what they are?

This starts with the letter A.

It doesn't weigh anything.
You can't see it,
but sometimes it has a

Smell.

Animals walking
on the ground,
birds flying high,

and some musical instruments use it.

Every living thing on
Earth
needs it.

It is all around you—
except under water.

You prefer it
fresh
and you
breathe
it in.

What is it?

air

Air is the mixture of different gases surrounding planet Earth. Humans and other animals breathe air into their lungs, and plants use it in photosynthesis.

Air becomes thinner with increasing altitude—very high up, air has so little oxygen that most people can only breathe with masks connected to oxygen tanks. Air can also carry various amounts of water vapor; on a really humid day, it might seem like you can feel the moisture in the air. The study of Earth's atmosphere, air, and oxygen is called "aerology," or "atmospheric science."

The word *air* can also be used in a few other ways. If plans are not settled, they could be described as "up in the air." A television show, when being broadcast, is said to be "on-air." And when many people sense something, it can be described as a feeling "in the air." You might say, "As summer vacation approached for the students, there was a great sense of anticipation in the air."

This starts with the letter B.

The faster you run,
the harder it is to catch.

When you are playing outside
on a cold day, you can see it but
not touch it.

You might be able to feel it on your face right before a dog licks you.

You can fog a mirror and fill a balloon with it. You can also use it to blow out candles on your birthday cake.

What could it be?

breath

Breath is the air that you take into and send out of your lungs when you breathe. Your lungs are designed to remove oxygen from the air you breath and transport it through your bloodstream to your muscles and organs, allowing you to jump, laugh, think, and climb a tree.

Breath can also be used figuratively. People might refer to something as "a breath of fresh air," meaning a welcome change. After a race you might say you are "out of breath," which means you are breathing very rapidly, trying to "catch your breath." And when something is beautiful, it can be said to "take your breath away," making you gasp with delight.

This starts with the letter C.

It can make a
liquid
turn into a
solid.

You might wish you felt
this in the middle of summer.

You can experience this
when sledding, building

a snowman,

or skiing down a mountain.

It makes you want to wear layers
of clothes and drink hot chocolate.

It can make you
shiver.

It is what you feel when
you reach into the freezer
or jump in an

icy lake.

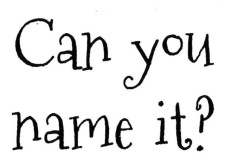

Can you
name it?

cold

The word *cold* describes a very low temperature that can be uncomfortable for humans. You might say that the pool was too cold for swimming, or the weather has been unusually cold this winter. Food can be too cold to eat, while lemonade on a hot summer day can be called nice and cold.

Cold can describe a person who isn't paying attention to you by giving you the "cold shoulder." *Cold* can also mean an infection. You might get the sniffles, a runny nose, or a fever: "I had aches and pains, but am finally getting over this cold!"

This starts with the letter D.

You can find this in a closet,
in a cave, and in a tunnel on the highway,
but you cannot feel it, taste it,
hear it, or smell it.

Some animals prefer it, and
some people are afraid of it.

It can seem mysterious.

This is what
shadows
are made of, but it can also
make them disappear.

When playing hide and seek at night,
a flashlight
or cell phone makes this go away.

But if you want to see stars,
you better make sure this is around.

It happens every day in most places
and tells you it is almost bedtime.

What is it?

darkness

Darkness is the state in which little or no light can be seen. You find your seat in the darkness of the movie theater, or find your way carefully in the darkness of a forest. *Darkness* can also refer to a color or shade that has more black in it than white. Some writers use darkness to convey mystery.

Nocturnal animals—animals that stay awake at night—have eyes that help them see in the dark. Cats are an example of nocturnal animals (but not dogs!). Humans can't see very well in darkness, unless they use special glasses called "night vision goggles."

This starts with the letter E.

It sounds exactly like someone's voice,
but there's no one there.

Sometimes, you can hear it from the other side of
a lake. Sometimes you can hear it in a place that's
hilly. And sometimes, you can hear it if you yell

down a well.

If you say, "Hello," it says, "Hello." And if you ask, "Who's there?" It asks, "Who's there?"

It's not a person hiding, and you can't find it even if you look—it's something you can't see.

But you can hear it—and when you do, it's always saying what you say.

WHAT IS IT?
What is it?
What is it?
What is it?

echo

You can hear an echo if you yell across a valley toward a mountain or in a really large room, like a gymnasium. An *echo* occurs when sound waves, such as your voice, bounce off of a surface and travel back to you. The distance between you and the surface determines how long it takes for the sound waves to travel back to your ears. The farther the distance, the longer it takes for you to hear an echo.

The word *echo* can also be used in other ways. When they agree with you, people sometimes say, "I echo what you just said." It can also mean repeating what another person says, echoing their words for emphasis.

This starts with the letter F.

You can't hold it.

If you try to catch it in your hands,
there's simply nothing there.

And you can't hear it.

You can often see it,
white as snowflakes or

gray as smoke,

floating around in

the sky.

Sometimes it has a damp and cold smell.

Your nose knows it's there
when you hike through it,
high on a mountain or through a
valley when the weather
conditions are just right.

It makes things harder to see, but you
can always see it when it drifts like

a cloud

and goes for a ride on the wind.

What can it be?

fog

Fog is a cloud made up of very tiny water droplets that float low in the air, making it hard to see. Weather conditions in the atmosphere have to be just right for fog to form. Mist is similar to fog, but it is not as heavy and does not obscure your eyesight. Both fog and mist can have a smell—damp and sometimes earthy.

Fog can also be used as a verb, such as when people say, "The car windshield fogged up," or as an adjective, such as when someone asks who took the last cookie and you say, "My memory of that is foggy."

This starts with the letter G.

You can't see, touch, smell,
taste, or hear it, but you feel
it when you try to jump high.

Because of this, apples fall to the
floor, an ice cream cone
drips onto your fingers, and
your feet stay on

the ground.

Sometimes, when you are
on a fun ride at an amusement
park or at the top of a swing,
you don't feel it for a moment.

And when you swim,
it seems to disappear completely.

Birds and airplanes
have to overcome it, and when

astronauts
are up in space,
they don't feel it at all.

What goes up must come down.

What is it?

gravity

Gravity is the force that draws a person or object toward the center of the earth. It's why food stays on your plate, and why your feet stay planted firmly on the ground. Gravity exists on all planets and stars, but its strength depends on their size and distance from other objects. If you jump as high as you can on Earth, you don't get very high. But on the moon, because there is less gravity, the same small jump turns into a giant leap.

Gravity keeps our planet spinning around the sun and pulls on clouds, affecting weather patterns. The moon's gravity causes the ocean tides on Earth to rise and fall. If it weren't for air, which creates resistance, a piece of paper and a piano dropped from the top of a building would both hit the ground at the same time because of gravity.

The word *gravity* comes from Latin and means "heavy" or "serious." People can also use the word *gravity* as a noun to refer to something important. You might say, "I did not understand the gravity of my actions until I accidentally broke the window."

This starts with the letter H.

You can't see it or hold it in your hands, but you can always sense when it's near you.

You can feel it on a
summer day
when you play in the
bright sunshine.

You can even feel it on a cold, snowy day if you bundle up in your snowsuit and mittens.

You can feel it when you stand close to
a fire.

And you can certainly feel it when you burn
your tongue with soup and say, "Ouch!"

What is it?

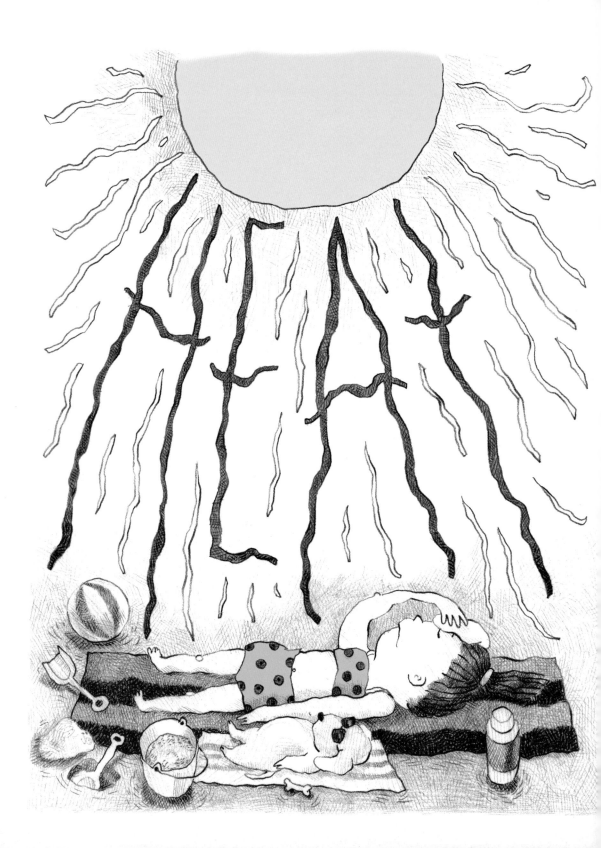

heat

When you come inside on a chilly day and go from feeling cold to feeling warm, you are feeling the effects of heat. A lit fireplace produces heat, as does your kitchen stove and radiator. You can feel heat in many ways: wearing layers of clothing, doing jumping jacks, and eating hot foods. And you can feel heat on a summer day when the sun is high overhead and there is no shade.

Heat originally comes from the German and Dutch languages and refers to the effect of warmth. *Heat* can be used in other ways too. It can capture anger. Two people might get in a "heated argument." As a verb, someone can "heat up" last night's leftovers. *Heat* can also describe the spiciness that chili peppers add to food. Finally, *heat* can refer to the preliminary or early races in a contest. You might say, "If you want to run in the championship race, you have to be one of the fastest runners in the earlier heats."

This starts with the letter I.

You cannot touch it,
but you can sure feel it.

A mosquito bite
can cause it, or you
can feel it because of
poison ivy.

A wool sweater or wool
socks make some people feel it.

When you get one of these,
it is impossible not to

scratch it.

Ah, that feels better...

What is it?

itch

We usually think of an *itch* as an unpleasant or irritating feeling on your skin that makes you want to scratch. Your back can itch, your nose can itch, and even the inside of your mouth can itch. Your eyes can burn and itch because of allergies, or after taking a dip in a swimming pool.

The word *itch* can also describe something you have a strong desire to do. You might be itching for a piece of apple pie, or be itching to go to the beach. In that case, you might persuade your family to load up the car with beach chairs, a cooler, and sand buckets, and head off to the shore to "scratch the itch." Bring along some apple pie and scratch two itches at once!

This starts with the letter J.

It makes you
Smile.

It's fun to remember one
and share it with a friend.

You can read one or
someone can tell you one.
Good ones make you
crack up.

Sometimes these can make you
laugh
so much your stomach hurts.

Have you heard a good one lately?

What could
it be?

43

Joke

A *joke* is something said or done to cause laughter and amusement. You can tell a joke to make people giggle, or you can play a harmless joke on someone by doing something like secretly stuffing toilet paper into the toes of their shoes.

Jokes make us laugh because of the unexpected. Based on past experience, we think we know the punch line or final result of the joke being told. But when the joke goes in an unexpected direction, our emotions suddenly flip-flop, and we end up perceiving this sudden change as humorous.

Two ducks are sitting on a pond. One of the ducks says, "Quack." The other replies, "I was going to say that!"

This starts with the letter K.

It is something you can feel
when it happens, but after it is over,
there is nothing left to touch, see, or hear.

It makes you happy.
Or it can
embarrass you,
making you blush.

Fathers and mothers
can give one to you.

So can a butterfly.

And you can give one to
your cat or dog, your mom
or dad, or your sister or brother.
You can even blow one across a room.

It can be quiet, or it can be a real
smacker.

You give one with your
lips

and it is full of
love.

Can you name it?

kiss

You show love by touching your lips to someone else's lips, cheeks, or head. You can also show happiness or gratitude by kissing other things too. A person whose dream has been to see another country might step off an airplane on arrival and kiss the ground. To show loyalty, people may kiss a king's ring. You can also blow someone a kiss by kissing the palm of your hand, putting your hand flat in front of your mouth, and blowing it toward them.

The word *kiss* can also be used figuratively. If you lose something, you might have to "kiss it goodbye." A weeping willow tree's branches might "kiss the ground," which means the branches are gently touching the ground. A basketball might "kiss the net" as it swishes through the basket, and a cat's paws might "kiss the grass" as it sprints across the backyard.

This starts with
the letter L.

People fall in it.

It goes with the thing
on the previous page.

Families feel it
for each other.
You can even feel
it for your pet.

It is a feeling in your

heart

that makes you
want to hug.

People say that it is what
makes the world go around.

It only has
four letters,
but it is the most powerful
force in the world.

**Can you guess
what it is?**

Love

love

Love is a feeling of strong affection. There are so many things you can love. You can feel love for your family, your friends, your pet, sports, food, and the beauty of nature.

The word *love* can also be used as an adjective—a musician can write a love song, or a poet can write a love poem. Grown-ups fall in love and sometimes get married. If people fall in love with each other when they first meet, it is called "love at first sight."

This starts with the letter M.

It lets you see and hear
things that happened
in the past.

It lets you

imagine

your breakfast from yesterday,
and your summer trip
from last year.

You make new ones every day,
and keep old ones

forever.

Everybody has this something.
You have one too.

What is
it called?

memory

Memory is made up of the different events—such as trips and adventures—that we remember and keep in our mind. Memories can be sad, happy, or neutral. You probably have powerful memories of what you did yesterday, last weekend, and even for your last birthday party. Some people even have photographic memories. If you memorize a poem or a speech, you are said to have "committed it to memory."

The word *memory* can also be used to talk about computers' and phones' capacity for storing lots of information.

This starts with the letter N.

It is something you can do during the day. When it is over, you can't feel, taste, or smell it.

Young children can find these annoying, and some adults dream about having as many as possible.

You can take one of these in

a hammock,

or you can take one in a bed with your cat or dog.

Sometimes your grandfather
can take one on a couch and

Snore.

What could
it be?

Z
Z
Z
Z

nap

Nap describes a short period of sleep, especially during the day. Some people awake from a nap rested and refreshed, while others wake up slowly and cranky. Everyone naps—babies, the elderly, teenagers, and adults.

The word *nap* can also be used figuratively, meaning you are not paying attention. You might say that the goalie is napping when a soccer ball gets by her. And you may not hear it very often, but *nap* is also used to describe a soft layer of threads on the surface of a piece of cloth, carpet, or other material. You might say that a velvet scarf is very soft and warm because it has a fuzzy nap.

This starts with the letter O.

This is a path along which objects travel.
Some are very short, and some are very long.

Each planet

has its own as it revolves around its sun, and our moon has one as it

revolves

around the Earth. But if an astronaut were to travel in a spaceship, she would not be able to touch it.

When the earth follows its own around the sun, it takes 365 days to complete.

What is it?

orbit

An *orbit* is the curved path that a planet, a moon, or a satellite follows as it goes around another object. Earth is in an orbit around the sun while the moon is in an orbit around Earth.

The word *orbit* is not only a noun, but also a verb. Satellites are launched into space to orbit the earth or other planets. And right here on Earth, electrons orbit around the nucleus of an atom. *Orbit* can also be used figuratively; two good friends who are in each other's orbit are always hanging around together.

This starts with
the letter P.

You can't taste, hear, or
smell it. You definitely
don't want to feel it!

When you get
your feelings hurt,
you experience it.

You feel this when you get a splinter,
have a headache, stub a toe, or
fall off your bike.

A broken arm
or a cut on your skin
also makes you feel it.

It can make you cry,
but it eventually goes away—
sometimes with the help
of some ice and a hug.

What
could it be?

pain

Pain is the physical feeling caused by an injury, a disease, or something else that hurts the body. A broken arm will cause you pain. You might feel a sharp pain when a doctor gives you a shot. Pain can also be emotional; you might feel pain from sadness when someone hurts your feelings.

Pain can be used figuratively to mean that something is bothersome. You might say that it is a pain to have to clean your room. A neighbor who uses your toys without asking might be said to be "a pain in the neck" because he annoys you.

This starts with the letter Q.

You can experience this
when you
sit by yourself.

You can discover this at night
when you are in bed.

You can find it
in the morning if you
are the first one in
the house to wake up.

It disappears when someone
says something, your dog

barks,

or your brother chews
his food loudly.

Silence

is very close to this,
and even a

whisper

makes this scurry away.

What is it?

quiet

Quiet is the absence of noise. There is quiet deep in the woods, in a library, or in your house at night when everyone is asleep.

Quiet can be used as a verb—you can quiet a crying baby— or an adjective—people can speak in a quiet voice. If a person does not speak very much, he might be described as quiet. *Quiet* can also mean calm, or not having much movement. The ocean can be quiet, and a bookstore without many shoppers can be having a quiet day.

This starts with
the letter R.

It looks just like you.
It wiggles its nose when you

wiggle your nose.

It smiles when you smile.
When you go away,
it goes away too.

By itself, it can't talk,
laugh out loud, or draw
with a crayon.

You can see it in

a rain puddle.

Sometimes you can see it in
a window
of a store.

You can see it when
you're combing
your hair in front of a
mirror.

It isn't really you,
but it belongs
to you and nobody else.

Can you guess
what it is?

reflection

Reflection is an image seen in a mirror or another shiny surface, such as a window, a lake, or a puddle. The word *reflection* can also mean something that shows the existence or character of something. You might say that having a big group of friends is a reflection of your cheerful personality, or an impressive art ability is a reflection of someone's creativity.

Reflection can also mean careful thought about something. After accidentally hurting a friend's feelings, you might spend time in quiet reflection. Or you might reflect on what a great summer vacation you had.

This starts with the letter S.

You can see it,
but you can't feel it or hear it.

Everybody has one.

You can't give it away
or use anyone else's.

It follows you wherever you go.

Sometimes it slides along
the ground. Sometimes it
walks along the wall next to you.
Sometimes it wiggles up the stairs
with you, wrinkling itself up
like a folded piece of paper.

It disappears on cloudy
days and in the dark.

It can be
black as coal,
and it's fun to step on.

When you do step on it,
you can't break it or hurt it.

What is it?

shadow

A *shadow* is the dark shape that appears on a surface when something stands between the surface and a source of light. A tree can cast a shadow across a lawn, and you can see your shadow on a sunny day.

The word *shadow* can also be used figuratively; a person might say that a town is located "in the shadow" of the Rocky Mountains, meaning it is close to the Rocky Mountains. *Shadow* is also used to convey a small amount. You might say that there is "not a shadow of doubt" that you can eat a whole pint of ice cream.

The word *shadow* can also be a verb that describes the process of following another person around to learn how to do their job. You could shadow your older cousin as she cuts lawns or babysits to earn money.

81

This starts with the letter T.

This is always passing by, but you can't see it, stop it, or even slow it down.

When you are raking leaves, cleaning your room, or waiting for your birthday to arrive,

it creeps by slowly.

But when you're happy
or playing excitedly with friends, it

flies by.

It sometimes makes you say,

"Just five more minutes."

You can measure it, but not with
a ruler or measuring tape.

Instead it is measured with
objects that hang on the wall,
are worn on the wrist,
or contained in a cell phone.

What is it?

time

Time is measured in seconds, minutes, hours, days, years, decades, and more. Time is always passing and sometimes, when it is passing very quickly, we say that "time flies." Time can refer to a particular time of the day—five o'clock—or it can refer to the part of a day, week, month, or year when something usually happens, such as *bath time*, *dinnertime*, or *playtime*.

You can "save time" or "waste time," or you can be "ahead of time" or "behind the times." *Time* can also be used as a verb. You use a stopwatch or your phone's timer to time the race or how long your friend can hang from the monkey bars.

This starts with the letter U.

This makes up
everything
around you, as far
as you can imagine.

And you are part of it.

Even though you cannot touch this,
it is filled with billions of objects.
Most of the objects are millions
and billions of miles away.

Earth is only a tiny part of it,
along with planets and comets,
moons and meteors, our sun and stars,
and the entire

Milky Way Galaxy.

Feeling
spacey?

If you go outside on a cloudless
night and look up, you can
see a small part of it.

What is it?

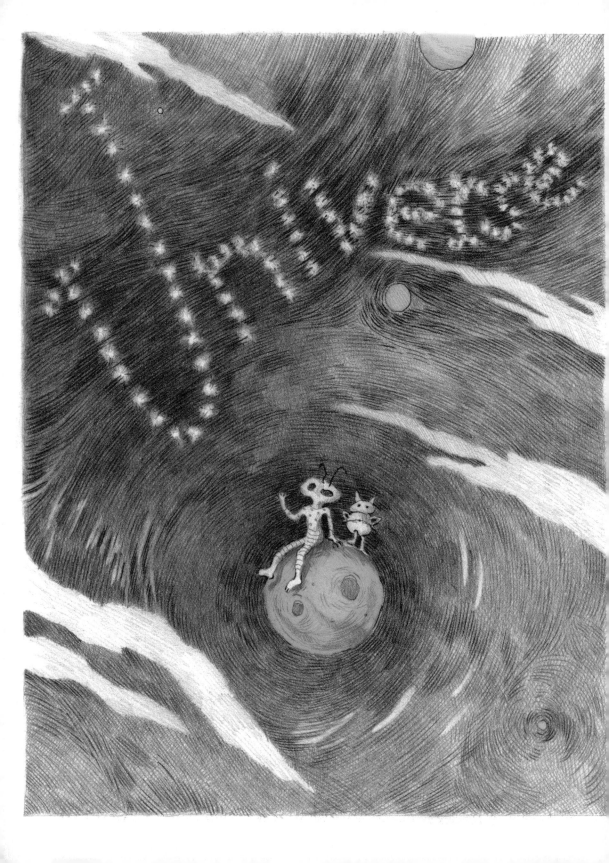

universe

The *universe* is all of space and everything in it, including stars, moons, Earth, all planets, galaxies, and our solar system. The universe is so vast that astronomers— scientists who study space—still have not found all the stars and planets that make up the universe. We don't even know how large our universe is!

Universe can also be used as a figure of speech referring to the people, places, and experiences that are associated with a particular person, place, or thing. You sometimes hear people say, for example, that a child is the center of a parent's universe, or Hollywood is the center of the filmmaking universe.

This starts with
the letter V.

Did you
hear
something?

You always have this
with you, but you are not
always allowed to use it.

Most people use it a lot
every day. It can be very high
or it can be very low—or
somewhere in between.

Adults
sometimes
ask you to
lower
it.

Babies have one,
and so do older people.
It allows you to
sing,
tell jokes, yell, and
talk.

Can you guess what it is?

Voice

Voice is the sound that comes out of your mouth and throat when you are speaking, singing, laughing, shouting, and whispering. People can have a deep voice, a quiet voice, or a loud, booming voice. If you shout too much or have a cold, you might lose your voice. If you are in a bad mood, your mother might say that she does not like the tone of your voice. If someone sings very well, they are praised as having a good voice. Speaking figuratively, shy people who finally speak up to express an opinion are said to have "found their voice."

Voice can also be a verb. Firefighters can voice concern about campfires in the woods, or you might voice a complaint about having to go to bed when your parents are downstairs with their friends.

This starts with the letter W.

You hear them every day, and
even though you can't catch them
or hold them, you can use them.

Some of them are very little:
shoe, in, is, fish, my, a.

Some of them are very big:

hippopotamuses,
thunderstorms,
stupefy,
Mississippi.

If you let the little ones play
together, they can sound like this:
A fish is in my shoe.

If you let the big ones line up in
a long parade, they can sound like this:
Thunderstorms stupefy
Mississippi hippopotamuses.

Some of them live in
books and newspapers,
where they don't make any sound at all.

When they're waiting for people to
use them, they sleep in dictionaries.

What are they?

words

Words are the meaningful sounds or combinations of sounds that we use to communicate. They are spoken or written.

Word can be used in a lot of different ways. *Word* can mean an order or command. You wait for your mother's word before eating, and an army begins marching when the captain gives the word. *Word* can describe news or information. You might await word on whether your favorite team won their game. *Word* can mean a promise to do something. You give your sister your word that you will help her with her homework.

There are also many figures of speech that use *word.* If another person tells someone something, the message is conveyed by "word of mouth." You are "at a loss for words" when you have nothing to say. If you say exactly what someone was thinking, they might respond by saying, "You took the words right out of my mouth!"

This starts with the letter X.

Kids trick-or-treating
sometimes dress up at
Halloween
to look like this.

Your luggage might get one of these at an airport before it's loaded onto an airplane.

If you hurt your leg, arm, hand, or some other part of your body, you go to the

doctor's office or hospital

to get one of these.

Make no bones about it,
this makes you look like

a skeleton.

What is it?

X-ray

X-ray is the image made when doctors and technicians use an X-ray machine to examine bones and organs inside a human or an animal. X-ray is actually a shorter term for X-radiation; radiation produces the black and white image of bones and organs. In 1895, when X-rays were discovered, the scientist was not sure how X-rays worked, so he added the "X" to show uncertainty.

X-ray can also be a verb. Doctors X-ray your hand or a dog's injured leg, and security X-rays your luggage at the airport.

This starts with the letter Y.

This is the name of a certain day.

Today, you have played, eaten,
laughed, hugged, and slept.
You will always have

memories

of what you did today.

But when you wake up

tomorrow

morning, the name of today will
have suddenly changed.

It is what
today
will be called
tomorrow.

What is it?

yesterday

Yesterday describes the day before today. You could say that yesterday's soccer game was canceled because of snow. And you can even be more precise and say you had pancakes for breakfast yesterday morning and ice cream after dinner yesterday evening.

Yesterday can also mean a time in the past. A television show about automobiles can show yesterday's cars as well as today's cars. A radio station might play yesterday's songs as well as new songs.

Figuratively, if a person is described as not being born yesterday, it means they are wise and cannot be easily fooled.

This starts with the letter Z.

This is nothing.

It is also the beginning of something,
or it can be the end of something.

When you have saved money
and then spend it all on a book
or candy, this is what you have left.

It divides
positive numbers
from
negative numbers.

It is the last thing
you say when you
are counting down
from 10, right before
"Ignition" and

"Blast off!"

What is this
thing that
isn't?

zero

Zero is represented by the figure 0 to mark the absence of quantity. Two minus two equals zero. *Zero* can also mean the temperature shown by the zero mark on a thermometer. A weather forecaster might say that the temperature will fall below zero tonight.

The word *zero* can also mean nothing at all. For example, some cars can go from zero to 60 miles per hour in five seconds. Or your distracted classmate's contribution to the class project was close to zero, meaning he did almost nothing to help.

Zero can also be used as a verb. You can be said to zero in on something, like your favorite word in this book, or that last piece of chocolate cake, which means you direct all of your attention to it.

About the Author

John Fixx lives in Connecticut and Vermont with his wife, Liza, and his children, Nat and Em, all of whom assisted with this book and have given him more puzzles, games, and mysteries than they know. A lifelong educator, John enjoyed working on this book, his first, with his Wesleyan University classmate, illustrator Abby Carter. This book began in 1959 by John's parents, author James Fixx and artist Mary Durling.

About the Illustrator

Abby Carter lives in Connecticut. When she is not illustrating, she is painting and drawing portraits of the guests at St. Vincent De Paul, a soup kitchen in Middletown, CT. Currently there are more than 200 of her portraits hanging on the walls.